T5-CRQ-863

WINDOW ON JAPAN: Japanese Children's Books and Television Today

WINDOW ON JAPAN:

Japanese Children's Books and Television Today

Papers from a symposium at the Library of Congress, November 18-19, 1987

Edited by Sybille A. Jagusch

Chief, Children's Literature Center~

Library of Congress Washington 1990

LIBRARY
COLBY-SAWYER COLLEGE
NEW LONDON, NH 03257

Z
1037.8
.J3
W56
1990

Cover and title page illustrations and other
decorative elements throughout the book are by
Mitsumasa Anno, from his book *Kirigami no
irasutorēshon* (Illustrations with paper cuts)
(Tokyo: Iwasaki Bijitsusha, 1976).
Used courtesy of the artist.

20994263

ACKNOWLEDGMENTS

The Children's Literature Center gratefully
acknowledges the following donors who
supported the symposium
"Window on Japan:
Children's Books and Television Today"

All Nippon Airways Co., Ltd.

Lloyd Cotsen, Los Angeles

The Japan Foundation

Setsutaro Kobayashi Foundation
Fuji Xerox Co., Ltd.

Library of Congress Cataloging-in-Publication Data

Window on Japan : Japanese children's books and television today :
    papers from a symposium at the Library of Congress, November 18-19,
    1987 / edited by Sybille A. Jagusch.
        p.   cm.
    ISBN 0-8444-0702-X
    ——— Copy 3. Z663 .W56   1990
    1. Children — Japan — Books and reading — Congresses.   2. Children's
literature, Japanese — Bibliography — Congresses.   3. Television
programs for children — Japan — Congresses.   I. Jagusch, Sybille A.
Z1037.8.J3 W56   1990
895.6'09282 — dc20

For sale by the Superintendent of Documents, U.S.
Government Printing Office, Washington, D.C.
20402.

⊗ The paper used in this publication meets the
minimum requirements of American National
Standard for Information Sciences — Permanence
of Paper for Printed Library Materials, ANSI
Z 39.48-1984.

108364

Contents

Preface

Children's books can be effective participants in the realm of international relations. Those of us in the children's book community who still work within the idealistic traditions established by the turn-of-the-century book women hold this belief, and the fourth symposium presented by the Children's Literature Center of the Library of Congress, "Window on Japan: Children's Books and Television Today," clearly confirms it.

During our preceding symposium, "Children, Science, and Books," in 1986, Dr. Lazer Goldberg of Hofstra University used the word *elegant* as a scientific term to describe the harmonious result of a mixture of ingredients. I want to borrow the expression to apply to the many ingredients that went into our Japanese symposium and its most elegant outcome.

I want to emphasize my appreciation to those who journeyed from the other side of the world to stimulate our thinking. They added Japanese grace and style to what they said, and, more importantly, through their sense of commitment they made apparent their emotional and intellectual involvement with the contemporary Japanese child. They gave us much more than information and expertise. They gave us a look into their minds, and we understood and were moved. For this beneficence I wish to thank Kyōko Matsuoka, Akiko Kurita, Tayo Shima, Mitsumasa Anno, and Kōichiro Noda.

My gratitude to the speakers goes beyond thanking them for their thoughtful papers. They also assisted us in so many other ways.

My special gratitude goes to Mrs. Shima, who assisted with fund-raising and numerous organizational matters, and to Mr. Anno, who gave us permission to reproduce paper cuts from his work *Kirigami no irasutorēshon.*

A special thank you goes to Dr. Thomas Rimer for providing the eloquent introduction to this volume. I wish also to acknowledge Ann Beneduce's fine contributions to the book. We could not reproduce here Mr. Anno's delightful slide presentation with which he amused us during the symposium, so his editor, who has worked with him on books published in this country, has recounted some of her experiences with Mitsumasa Anno for us.

I would also like to extend my appreciation to Evelyn Sinclair, the Children's Literature Center's editor in the Library's Publishing Office, for her professionalism, guidance, and support.

In retrospect I realize that the symposium left us with sharpened perceptions, not the least of which came from the satisfaction derived from goals shared and the heightened awareness of our common humanity. While the Library of Congress provided the Window on Japan, our guests reciprocated by giving us a comprehensive and unclouded view through that window.

SYBILLE A. JAGUSCH
Chief, Children's Literature Center

Introduction

All those who attended the delightful and thought-provoking symposium on Japanese children's literature held at the Library of Congress on November 18–19, 1987, of which the present volume provides a highly useful record, took away a number of strong personal impressions concerning the importance of children's literature to every growing generation, a conviction that surely developed in response to the enthusiasm and graciousness of the various speakers, whose sense of occasion and dedication to their subject gave their remarks a special significance.

I myself, who have been a student of Japanese literature and culture for some twenty-odd years, was struck anew with the vigor, charm, and vitality of the best of the children's literature produced in that country. In the kind of representative works discussed in the symposium and listed in the bibliography in the beautiful publication *Japanese Children's Books at the Library of Congress* (1987), the companion volume to this collection of essays, there is consistently revealed an artistry and a sense of communion between the writer and his or her readers that suggests a very special, close, and positive relationship. There is little talking down to youngsters in these books, little in the way of forced over-simplifications. Those readers are treated as real lovers of the printed word, albeit younger ones, who can be seen to be potentially as open to the excitements and puzzlements of the whole range of human experience as any adult. We use the phrase *children's literature;* in the Japanese case, the emphasis is on the noun, not the adjective. These books are most often works of literature that happen to be written with children in mind. Those who read them are thus both given a challenge and paid an important compliment.

Why should this be so? One reason, I think, is that many fine modern writers in Japan have never sought to specialize, seeking rather to address some of their works to adults, some to children. This has been particularly true of some of the best of the modern Japanese poets. Kitahara Hakushū (1885–1942), for example, perhaps the most imaginative avant-garde poet of his period, mixed in his verse remarkable images from a variety of literary traditions and took the French Symbolist poets as his spiritual mentors. Yet in the midst of these experiments, he also wrote children's poems of surprising ease and grace. Miyazawa Kenji (1886–1933), who lived in the remote regions of northern Japan and achieved a remarkably effective evocation of Buddhist metaphysics in his dazzling longer poems, created as well droll and poetic stories for children still as popular now as they were when first published in the 1920s; indeed, his prodigious fame in Japan is firmly based on both. Ogawa Mimei (1882–1961), a committed writer of humanistic inclinations, who often took as his subject the poor and oppressed of his generation, created along with those writings some of the great classics of modern Japanese children's literature, beginning with his *Red Boat* of 1910.

A second reason for this commitment by many first-class modern Japanese writers to compose works for children involves, I think, a powerful urge to discover or, often, rediscover the past, and then attempt to convey a sense of that past to the next generation. By the turn of the century, when more and more Japanese were moving to the cities and old customs were being lost, young intellectuals like Yanagida Kunio (1875–1962) began collecting folktales and writing them down, so constructing a vision of the past from rural areas, where myth, legend, and history often intertwined. Yanagida's stories and tales have delighted and fascinated young readers ever since he began to publish them in accessible versions for the general public. In the postwar period, the great modern playwright Kinoshita Junji (born 1914) attempted in some of his dramas to use in a new fashion some of these old stories in order to reveal what he felt were the deepest, and the truest, levels of myth capable of revealing the essential qualities inherent in Japanese culture. His 1949 play *Yūzuru* (Evening crane), in which a peasant marries a magical bird who looks after him until, in his greed, he begins to exploit her, remains perhaps the most popular

Japanese modern drama written since that time. Yet Kinoshita is as much admired for his children's books as for his plays. Indeed, his children's stories may have earned a greater readership, since they circulate all over the country, while his dramas can only be experienced, on the stage at least, in the larger urban areas.

All of these important writers, and many more, are listed in *Japanese Children's Books at the Library of Congress.* Their presence there, it seems to me, stands as proof that, in the Japanese context, literature is considered as a part of everyone's mental and spiritual life, whatever the reader's age. The unity of feeling this fact suggests, and the respect that young readers are thus meant to receive, has long provided a heartening

context in which to write children's literature in Japan. Fortunately, as more and more representative works are translated into English, all of us are able to learn just how beguiling this special tradition can be.

J. Thomas Rimer

The Japanese Child in a Changing World

by KYŌKO MATSUOKA

Here at the Library of Congress I feel almost at home. Washington is so close to Baltimore, and Baltimore's Enoch Pratt Free Library is my "home" as far as my professional career is concerned. It was there that I got my first job as a children's librarian, and far more important than that, it was there that I equipped myself with what was to serve as the backbone of my professional self. I owe much in this regard to the late Edwin Castagna, then director of the library, to Isabella Jinnette and Barbara Moody, of the Office of Work with Children, to Margaret G. Cook, my branch librarian, and to many others who taught me, both by words and by example, what librarianship stands for.

I have never forgotten what Mr. Castagna said to us, the newly employed, on our first day at the library. It was right after the Labor Day weekend in 1962. He said, "We belong to a group of people who believe in the goodness of books. It is our duty and our joy to draw more people into this group." How many times, during the twenty-five years that followed, have I gone back to these quiet words of his to clarify the purpose of my work and to encourage myself!

I said "twenty-five years." It is hard to believe that a quarter of a century has passed since that day and that I am here today to share with you what I have experienced during that period working with children and books in Japan. Now what have I done in these years?

For the first two and a half years after I returned home from the United States, I worked at the Osaka Municipal Central Library. Then, in 1967, I opened in my house in Toyko a small children's library, or a *bunko,* a word you are probably familiar with by now. Later in 1974 the bunko was incorporated with another three bunkos, including Miss Momoko Ishii's Katsura Bunko, which was founded as early as 1958, to be accredited by the Educational Commission of the Tokyo Metro-politan Government. This incorporated, accredited bunko is one of the few private children's libraries in the country, and the only one of its kind in Tokyo.

The Tokyo Children's Library, as it is called, now has a small children's room and a small research library, both open to the public. We also have a small publishing department which publishes a quarterly journal, *Kodomo Toshokan* (Children's libraries), featuring book reviews. Our research library has a special collection of books that have been awarded various children's book awards and prizes in postwar Japan. Based on this collection, we compile and publish a comprehensive reference book on the Japanese children's book awards every five years.

From the time of its establishment, the library has placed a special emphasis on promoting storytelling. It has conducted regular courses and occasional workshops on the subject and has published a series of booklets about storytelling that also contain stories good to tell. Along with my work as the director of this library, I have taught children's literature and library work in several colleges and universities, have translated a number of English and American children's books into Japanese, and have written a few children's books myself.

All of this has kept me fully occupied. Very fortunately, however, I could continue to have direct contact with children, in spite of all the other work I have to do, because I had this little bunko in my own house. Every Saturday for the past twenty years, I have spent the whole afternoon with the children in this very informal little library, telling stories to them, reading aloud for the young ones and talking with the older ones. This is the portion of my work that I have enjoyed most, and I used to call my bunko my class-room, for I could learn a lot about children and their relationship with books in this narrow space. What I am going to relate this morning is all based on my experiences there, especially the part that deals with children.

If I had to choose one word to sum up the past quarter of a century, the word would be *change*. For us this has been a time of sudden and overwhelming change — with changes that came to us like great big surging waves. From the point of view of children's reading, some of the changes were certainly to be welcomed, for instance, the increase of reading facilities. Public libraries in Japan have tripled during this period. Take for example the Osaka Municipal Library where I once worked. In 1962, there were only three libraries in the city — one central, one branch, and one reading room — serving a population of nearly three million people. Now, with a slightly decreased population, the city has twenty-two libraries, with at least one branch in every ward.

More noteworthy than the number, however, is the change in the concept of public library service. Traditionally it was understood that the primary function of a library was to preserve materials. Little attention was paid to using them for the benefit of the general public. For ordinary people, twenty-five years ago, a public library was nothing but a place of study for young students. Seats, rather than books, were in demand. The Osaka Municipal Central Library was proud of its huge study hall with a capacity of eight hundred seats. It was the rule then that only the number of patrons equal to the seating capacity were allowed to enter the library. The rest had to wait at the entrance standing in a queue. Often on weekends and during school holdiays the queue became quite long. At one time, I saw that the children waiting outside the building greeted those who came out of the library with loud clapping of hands, for this meant their turn was near!

Obviously the library was not encouraging people to borrow books then. Only popular fiction and children's books were circulated. The borrowers had to go through a long and complicated procedure to get a library card that would only allow them to take one book at a time for a week. No wonder the total circulation of the whole library that year was about fifteen thousand, whereas in 1986 the city's libraries circulated more than 4.4 million books altogether.

Change in the concept of a public library can also be seen in the choice of sites for new library buildings. Whereas the old libraries were located in a park away from the hustle and bustle of a town, the new ones, trying to be easily accessible to citizens, have been established in housing developments, near a local station, or even in a corner of a market. Certainly the past quarter of a century is to be remembered as the era in which our public libraries have become, for the first time in our history, a part of the everyday life of the ordinary people. And throughout the country, half of the users of public libraries are children.

Besides public libraries, there are bunkos in Japan to promote books to children. A bunko is a mini-library operated by either individuals or groups, usually mothers, for the purpose of providing better reading materials for children. The idea was started by a handful of people in the 1950s, grew steadily in the 1960s, and spread widely in the 1970s. Osaka, with about four hundred bunkos in the area, is known for its vigorous bunko activities.

The earlier bunkos were usually housed in private homes and run by individuals, but the later ones were often located in community centers and managed cooperatively by groups of volunteers. Sometimes these two types of bunkos are differentiated, the former as a *home bunko* and the latter a *community bunko*. Regardless of the type, however, they all have in common the fact that they are private and voluntary efforts to make books available to children. Because of the devotion of numerous mothers who took part in this activity, the bunko has grown to be a major influence in the realm of children's reading in our country.

Attempts have been made to analyze the reasons behind the development of this unique movement. Some find an explanation in the paucity of public libraries or in the great interest our parents took in children's reading. Others give credit to such people as Miss Momoko Ishii, Miss Yoshiko Kogouchi, or Mr. Shogo Saito, for their leadership and inspiration. In addition to these reasons, which are all valid, I would like to indicate three more factors which I think are worthy of attention.

First, one aspect of the bunko movement involves women's participation in social activities. With the availability of electric appliances and the change of lifestyle, many housewives, especially in urban areas, found themselves liberated from domestic tasks, with surplus energy and time on one hand and the desire to do something worthwhile outside the home on the other. The bunko offered just the right kind of opportunity for them. Bunkos have something to do with children, who are the primary concern of these women, and in them their experiences and knowledge as mothers can be put to good use. Moreover, the work is very rewarding. Behind the widespread development of community bunkos in the 1970s lies this element, I think.

Second, the bunko movement has an aspect of anti-school-education sentiment. It is true that a public library itself, being an institute of informal education, has in its nature the possibility of counteracting the formal quality of education. Even more so does the bunko, which is privately financed and managed by volunteers. To let children encounter books in a *free* atmosphere was the basic idea of the bunko, free from schools and free from grades.

Then in the 1970s our schools found themselves confronted with various difficult problems, such as violence, bullying, children suffering from school phobia, or children committing suicide. The countermeasure most of the schools unfortunately took was enforcing stronger control over children. Bunko mothers, perhaps more instinctively than consciously, felt the danger of this, and their desire to secure for children a place where they could be free from the pressure of studies, of competition, and of uniformity of values served as the driving force for the bunko activities. Recently several bunkos began to offer children various non-book-related programs, such as hiking or camping, cooking, crafts, simple scientific experiments, or just the playing of games. In a way these activities are an attempt to let children have fun and thus to invigorate them. Intentionally or not, bunkos are serving as little windows to let a bit of fresh air into children's lives,

otherwise too rigidly controlled by the schools.

Third, we must not forget that the children's books themselves inspired the pioneering mothers, and their genuine interest in contemporary children's literature has sustained their enthusiasm in the movement. The mothers, especially those who started bunkos in the 1960s, had as children never read the kind of children's books the bunkos could offer. How fresh and enthralling the books looked to them, when they first came to know them! They enjoyed them thoroughly themselves, and the pleasure sent them to share the joy with the young.

Now this third aspect leads us on to the other favorable changes in the world of children's reading of the past two decades, that is, the improvement in the quality of children's books. The past two decades, especially the 1960s, were a period of marked importance as far as our modern juvenile publishing is concerned. It is in this period that the bulk of what we consider the standard children's books were published and that most of our writers and illustrators now nationally and internationally known began to work.

Two factors contributed to this, I think. One is the influence of foreign children's books and the other is the devoted efforts of our book people. Toward the end of the 1950s, works by such authors as Erich Kästner, Astrid Lindgren, and Eleanor Farjeon began to be translated and introduced to our readers. Rosemary Sutcliff, Philippa Pearce, Otfried Preusler, and Beverly Cleary followed. Fantasy by C. S. Lewis and J. R. Tolkien particularly attracted our readers. In the field of picture books, the major works of Virginia Lee Burton, Robert McCloskey, H. A. Rey, Marie Hall Ets, and later Maurice Sendak were introduced successively. All of these works have been for us such a potent influence as to change the very concept of children's literature for our people.

Then there were the book people in Japan — the publishers, editors, writers, and illustrators who had been waiting for the time to be ripe. Having experienced the disasters of the war, they were firmly determined to devote themselves to the cause of children's books. The late Mr. Teiji Seta, a writer, translator, researcher, and educator, who contributed more than anybody else to the enrichment of children's literature in postwar Japan, confided to me once, not long after the end of the war, "Now that I am liberated, I must release all of my ability and time to children, for they are our hope for the future." The same philosophy is expressed in the message conveyed in the publication of the Iwanami Shonen Bunko, or the Iwanami Boys' Library, a famous series in which most of the translated works mentioned above first appeared. It reads: "Upon our completely demolished land, grass grows. From our burned-down trees, buds shoot out. Those fresh signs of life teach us what to value and whom to respect. Our

hope and future lie in our boys and girls. They are the green leaves of grass and fresh sprouts of trees of our country. The purpose of this series is none other than to offer them bright sunshine and abundant water that will nurture their minds. . . ."

The very tone of the sentence tells us about the kind of sentiment with which those people tackled their work. The time helped, and of course, the economic growth made it possible. Hence the richness of good books in the 1960s. The good time was short-lived, however. As juvenile publishing became a prosperous business, things began to change again very quickly.

The enriched juvenile publications invited changes in the attitude toward children's books held by the general public. For the first time since the Meiji Restoration, adults began to admit the value and meaning of books for sheer pleasure. Before, books had

to teach; they had to be of use. Although this didactic approach is still strong, appearing time and again under thin disguise, more and more people find release in children's books. At least it has become an established attitude of parents nowadays that reading *is* very important. This is itself a great change if we consider the prewar days when common people thought reading something wasteful, or even harmful. Book-loving children often had to hide to read. Now no parents would complain that their youngsters read. On the contrary, "My daughter reads nothing but comics," or "Our son won't touch a page of the books I have purchased for him," would be typical complaints of our parents today.

Books became easily available. Their quality improved. The attitude of adults toward children's reading was encouraging. . . . It sounds as if we had everything we could hope for, as far as the environment for children's reading is concerned. What an irony it is then that children, the very readers, began to change, and in an undesirable way, too!

In the very beginning of the 1970s, I began to notice the changes in children. They became more conspicuous as the years passed and reached their worst at the end of that decade. In discussing the changes that appeared in our children, I will intentionally avoid giving you either very generalized information or statistics. Instead I will give you a few sketches of children in my own library. I think they reflect fairly well what was happening to all of our children in our country.

The first phenomenon that struck me was that children were not looking into my eyes as they used to while listening to my stories. They either looked down or let their eyes roam about aimlessly. This made me quite uncomfortable, as I felt I had lost the thread that tied me to my listeners. It was quite symbolic, when I look back on the situation now, that the first change happened to the very base of communication: eye contact.

Then we began to notice that children were no longer developing particular attachments to the books they liked. Before, once they had found what they liked, children would stick to the same title. One boy checked out *Choo Choo* nine times in succession, and worried his mother, who suspected that her son had a monomanic tendency. A little girl of five liked *Guri and Gura* very much. She demanded that I read it to her every time she came, and this lasted for eighteen months! Then the change came. In the 1970s children seemed to be reading this and that haphazardly, always going after new books, seldom returning to the old and familiar. Often they were not willing to read sequels — even if they liked the first one — which we found very hard to understand.

The tendency was also observed in children's re-

sponses to the stories told. Before, children used to love to listen to their favorites over and over again. Sometimes I got a loud chorus of "Tell it again!" the moment I finished the story. Hardly did we get such enthusiastic responses any more. When I asked children, "Is there any story you'd like to hear once again?" they would politely answer, "Not particularly."

They did not appreciate repetition within a story either. Most of the popular folktales have repetition and that was one element children enjoyed most before. Now many children apparently got bored when the second and third prince went through the same stage of adventure as the first one. I could feel the air become dull and the children's minds begin to wander.

We also began to notice that children seemed to forget what they had read, and quite easily, too. We still use the old-fashioned charging system in which children have to write their names on bookcards. We were dismayed by children who came to the charging desk, took out the bookcard, and found their names on it in their own writing.

At one time, a boy asked my fellow librarian if she could help him find an interesting book. She introduced him to *The Lion, the Witch, and the Wardrobe*, telling the first part of the story. The boy listened as if fascinated. "I'll take that," he said. Then at the charging desk, he looked at the bookcard and said "Ah, I've read this one," finding that he had checked out the book only a few weeks before! How can one read and forget a book like this? Isn't childhood the most impressionable time of our life? Aren't we working hard because we believe that the books anyone reads as a child will have a deep and lasting effect on him or her? We were quite shocked by this incident.

Another sad change was that we found children laughed less over the funny stories we told at Story Hour. The same story that once sent children rolling all over the floor with laughter now provoked only a slight loosening of cheek muscles. Especially nonsense stories like *The Old Woman and Her Pig* seemed to have lost their magic. We recognized that children's taste was becoming more and more sophisticated. Children were no longer naive, as we wished them to be, yet they were immature in many other ways compared with children of the same age several years before.

All in all, our children were not getting as much fun from the books they read as they used to, it appeared to me. Before, a boy would say, "Gee, that was good!" with such warmth, when he came to return the books. Now children hardly said anything, and if we pushed a little and asked, "How was it?" they would say, "Yeah, it's O.K." But we missed that childlike enthusiasm in their voices, which was once very familiar to our ears.

Indeed our teachers and parents today express their concern about the fact that young ones nowadays are not wide-eyed, not easily interested, and very hard to move. I wonder if this is because children have developed a sort of self-defense mechanism against too many stimuli or too strong a stimulus. Most likely they are protecting themselves from overwhelming stimuli by trying not to get themselves too deeply or too seriously involved with what is in front of them. The attitude thus formed is shown in reading. We cannot blame children for that, though, when we look at their life today.

No doubt children became busy, extremely busy. Their time was calculated and scheduled. When I opened my bunko twenty years ago, we didn't have a clock in the room, but nobody missed it. Children seemed to have all the time there was to themselves. Then in 1977, when I had my house rebuilt and the library moved into a new room, I was annoyed by the fact that so many children asked us what time it was. We simply had to have a clock in the room. It is amazing, too, that the time unit has now become so minute. Children nowadays say something like, "At 2:25 I must leave here for the piano lesson," or "I can stay here until ten minutes to four." *Juku* (a special after-school program for supplementary studies), swimming clubs, ballet lessons, art classes, abacus schools, and all the other extra activities are cutting their days and weeks into pieces.

So children are tired. They often say, "I'm tired" as though it were some kind of greeting. That our children are so busy with extracurricular activities may be a result of our parents' overheated education-consciousness. We feel that children are under the very strong control of their parents, especially their mothers. For example, before, we used to have more children in the library on rainy days, for the simple reason that they could not play outdoors. Now when the weather is bad, we have hardly any children. We can almost hear their mothers saying, "Let's not go to the library today, because it's raining." With an average of 1.7 children in a family, our children are rarely left on their own. Their twenty-four hours are carefully traced and managed by mothers, if not by schools.

One of my fellow librarians once asked a five-year-old, "Well, Noriko, what kind of books do you like?" "Ask Mommy," was her answer. "No, I don't mean what *your mother* likes. I want to know what *you* like." Then the little girl said, "Yes, I know what you mean. But Mommy can answer it better, 'cause she knows my life history far better than I do!"

Then there is television. When people discuss the problems of children today, they never fail to point out the strong influence exerted by television upon children. When it comes to the problem of reading, a lot of people criticize television for damaging our children's reading habits and reading ability. I do not deny that as a single factor television has had the most extensive influence. The changes in the relationship between children and books that I have just described all happened after television had spread to almost 100 percent of our families, and babies began to grow up with it. It is true that television is taking up a good part of our children's leisure time, which might otherwise be spent in reading. True also perhaps is that children who are accustomed to the speed and sensation of television programs might find reading a tedious process.

These things, however, are not what concerns me most about television in connection with children's reading. What troubles me is the question of television affecting children's language-learning process. To be more precise, while it is a fact that for many children the initial images that they associate with words are often those of television, isn't it also true that television influences the quality of the images children create within themselves as they read?

The other day I read an interesting article in a newspaper written by one of our writers on this subject. He tells about an incident that had happened when he took his three-year-old daughter to the sea for the first time. "Look, dear, that's the ocean!" he said to her, excited at the thought that this was to be her first encounter with the "real" ocean. For a moment, the little girl looked puzzled. Then she cried, as if she comprehended, "Yes, Daddy, I know. This was once on TV, wasn't it?" The little Miss Know-It-All-by-TV! She was neither awed nor overwhelmed!

For the generation of people who are exposed to television after they grow up, what television offers is a pseudo-reality, or vicarious and extended experiences. But for children who are constantly exposed to television from infancy, real experiences often come to them after the television images. Thus children acquire a good part of their vocabulary by primarily associating television images with words. And television images are largely visual, seldom or never involving other senses such as smell, sound, touch, or feel. The images thus acquired tend to be superficial, and perhaps appeal more to our intellect than to our emotions. Our children's inability to enjoy the same familiar story repeatedly may have something to do with this. I wonder whether a story for them isn't reduced to information to know and no longer regarded as a drama that they themselves might relive.

We know that reading is an act of creating images within oneself, evoked by the words one reads. If the contents of a child's "words" are largely produced by television and not backed up by his own experiences, it is only natural that his reading does not call forth powerful and persuasive pictures in his mind, and his senses and emotions are not stimulated. Here is perhaps one clue to understanding the weakened relationship of children to books.

If I were to describe a modern Japanese child in a somewhat exaggerated way, it would be like this: The child is well fed and wants nothing in the way of materialistic things. He is given ample opportunity and impetus for education but little time and freedom for inner growth. Words he knows many of, but their value for him grows relatively weaker. He is constantly under pressure, striving ever so hard to adjust himself to live up to the expectations of parents and school, and he is very much exhausted. . . .

The changes in children are a manifestation of the highly complex changes of the time: urbanization, changes in industry, change in family structure — with the increased importance of nuclear families and the decrease of the number of children in a family — the spread of automation and highly technical methods of communication, and the rapid economic growth that lies behind it all. As a result, the speed of life has accelerated. People have become restless. Moreover, the general atmosphere of the time is full of uncertainty, of fear and doubt. All of this has affected us adults and is reflected in our children. What I find ironical is that the same factors that brought forth favorable changes in outer conditions for children's reading also worked to create inner problems for our young readers.

I must hasten to say, though, before you have too dark an image of Japanese children settled in your mind, that things began to change again in the 1980s. As far as we can see in our library, children seem to be recovering composure. They are no longer as restless as they were as the 1970s came to an end. Their responses to stories told are turning to positive ones, and their power of concentration is strengthened. We welcome these changes, though we cannot yet identify the reasons for them. I have a suspicion that this has much to do with the slowed-down economy. If so, we have much to look forward to!

I have to confess that there have been times when I was very much depressed. So many things were happening to our children in such a short time that we felt quite helpless. I guess we were being rolled and whirled under the big wave of change. Now that the first big wave has passed, I feel as if I have come up to the surface to get a breath. Difficult situations remain, and there will be further changes in the future. Nevertheless I am determined to be hopeful. Having gone through the time of dazzling changes, I have learned to look at things in the long perspective and not be easily discouraged.

On the surface, children do look different. But in them there is something that remains unchanged. The fact that they need books and that books can fulfill their needs does not change.

Just a week ago, one of my staff read a picture book titled *Who Sings the Lullaby?* to a little seven-year-old girl. The text is written in verse and it goes like this:

> Hush — a baby seal is about to sleep.
> Seals sleep by the sea,
> While waves are dancing
> And dancing around them.
>   Alas, nobody is going to sing a lullaby for him.
> . . .
> Hush — a lion cub is about to sleep.
> Lions sleep in the desert,
> While winds are whistling
> And whistling around them.
>   Alas, nobody is going to sing a lullaby for him.

It goes on like this with the baby bear, hare, beaver, squirrel, and so on, until it comes to:

> Hush — a human baby is about to sleep.
> He sleeps in bed.
> Is somebody going to sing a lullaby for him?
> Yes, "Nen-nen-yo, nen-nen-yo,"
> His mother sings a lullaby for him.
> Yes, "Nen-nen-yo, nen-nen-yo,"
> His father sings a lullaby for him.

When the reading was over, this little girl put her arms around the neck of the librarian and whispered, "Isn't it wonderful to be a human being!"

It is at such a moment that we feel grateful to be children's librarians. This is the moment when our belief in the goodness of books and of children is reinforced.

Well, this has been a quick and very simplified survey of children's reading in Japan for the last quarter of a century. As it turned out, it is also a brief report of a children's librarian, trained in the United States, on how she has tried to put what she had learned into practice in Japan. Therefore I humbly and respectfully submit this to those who have helped me to pursue this profession, and to all of you here, who, I am sure, belong to that same group of people who believe in the goodness of books. Thank you.

Postwar Children's Book Publishing: Its Turning Points

by AKIKO KURITA

"Why have Japanese publishers stopped buying picture book translation rights from us lately?" This is a question frequently asked by foreign publishers these days at the book fairs. The question is related to the boom in children's picture books, especially translated works, of some years ago.

If you look at the table of statistics for the past seventeen years (1970–86) that I have prepared, you will find that the figures for children's books are increasing rather than decreasing (see p. 25). Again, you may well ask, "Why?" These are complicated questions, but if you are patient enough to follow my explanation to the end, you may find the answer.

I tried to begin with figures from 1945, from right after the war, but I found that these figures are rather confusing. In some years, reference books are counted as children's books. Comics with less than three months of consignment sales are categorized as magazines, but those with more than six months are counted as "children's books/social science" or sometimes "art."

Nevertheless, these figures and names of publishers may help clarify the situation.

In botanical terms, the Japanese children's book field after World War II might be categorized as follows:

1945	Dormant period: seeds are still under the ground owing to a serious paper shortage.
1946–1950	Embryo period: seeds begin to sprout.
1951–1965	The saplings grow to trees.
1966–1980	Overdevelopment: too many trees are yielding too much fruit.
1981–1987	Turning point: trees will continue to grow as healthy trees or they will wither.

These stages may be observed in social phenomena, as well as in the gradual changes in distribution channels for children's books.

From 1946 on, new picture magazines for kindergarten-age children began to appear and others that had ceased publication during the war were revived. Also, some major publishers began issuing new story magazines for children from the primary school to the high school level. For these periodicals, well-known established writers wrote short stories mainly on subjects drawn from daily life. At that time, regular literary production for adults had yet to recover from wartime setbacks, so many "adult" authors wrote children's stories for a living. Michio Takeyama's *Biruma no Tategoto* (The harp of Burma), a typical work from this era, was written as a requiem for the author's students who had served at the front in the war in Burma. In *Nijushi no Hitomi* (Twenty-four eyes), the woman writer Sakae Tsuboi wrote a realistic novel based on the wartime life of a country school teacher which was also welcomed by the public. Both works were adapted for film and radio, and they are still being read by children as well as adults today.

In 1946, the Japanese Association of Writers for Children was formed by twenty leading children's book authors. It has now grown to a membership of more than six hundred. The aim of the association is to encourage the creation of democratic children's literature and to promote works upholding its ideals.

In 1949 Shincho-Sha introduced world-famous children's books such as *Heidi* and *The Yearling* to Japan, but after three years they stopped publishing children's books and concentrated their efforts on literature for adults. About this time, mass-market publishers also began to revive their activities. One of these was *Shogakukan,* which means "House for Primary School Children." Shogakukan was an early publisher of elementary-grade-level monthly magazines carrying information, stories, comics, games, and other articles suitable for children for each primary school grade. When some firms retreated from the grade-level magazine field a few years later, Shogakukan and Gakken (an abbreviation for *Gakushu Kenkyu Sha,* meaning "Learning and Studying") remained active and are still active today.

Television was first introduced in Japanese homes in 1953 and gradually the influences of TV broadcasting began to spread. Following the grade-level magazines for children, other publishers launched similar types of magazines, attaching supplements which attracted children — sometimes supplements that were larger than the magazines themselves. Comic cartoon supplements became extremely popular, giving rise to the so-called "war over the comics." In the end, the story magazines were pushed out of the market by the comics. As a result of TV broadcasting, a whole variety of illustrated information books were published, to appeal to people who were especially attracted to visual presentations.

In a way, 1953 was an epoch-making year for children's picture books in Japan. Iwanami Shoten, an old and established publisher, started introducing foreign titles, mainly from the United States and England, as a series in uniform format, together with original Japanese works. These translations included books such as *The Story of Little Black Sambo,* by Helen Bannerman, *The Little House,* by Virginia Lee Burton, *Curious George Takes a Job,* by H. A. Ray, and *The Story of Ferdinand,* by Munro Leaf and Robert Lawson. Many of these were from the classic picture book period of the 1930s and 1940s. Until that time, most picture book illustrations drawn by Japanese artists had tended to be static tableaux, without much movement in the pictures. Therefore, those vividly drawn pictures attracted writers and critics of children's books, and appealed to teachers and mothers, as well as children.

Inspired by Iwanami Shoten's newly introduced picture books, Fukuinkan Shoten (meaning "Gospel House"), a bookstore in Kanazawa, started a monthly series of softcover picture books, each containing one story, for Protestant kindergartens and nursery schools. The motto of Tadashi Matsui, then editor-in-chief, was to express stories through pictures. He was opposed to the idea of picture books merely as digests of famous stories in the form of picture albums. The content of the Fukuinkan picture books varied from original stories, folktales, or informative books to books on daily life. The idea behind them came from the Père Castor Albums of France. Since then, many outstanding picture books have been introduced.

A new Library Law was set up in 1953, stipulating that each school should have its own library, and by April 1954 most schools did have one. But this did not — and does not — mean the schools received financial support for libraries from the Ministry of Education.

In the same year the Association of Children's Book Publishers was formed to coordinate publishers' various activities, including promotion to school libraries. And we cannot forget the campaign "twenty minutes reading time with mother and children" initiated by Hatoju Muku, a distinguished children's book author, or the home library campaign.

The year 1955 marked Japan's entry into a period of

great economic development. While fathers were busy in their companies, mothers in the home devoted themselves to the education of their children. Advances in women's higher education caused the number of female teachers to increase. The selection of books for children was therefore largely in the hands of women, who tended to choose beautiful picture books, fairy tales, and the like. On the other hand, they did not choose as often the more serious books or adventure stories that appeal to boys. To encourage the creation of better books for children, a number of prizes were established in 1955 by public and private organizations.

This year was also a landmark in the development of Japanese children's literature, for, with Satoru Sato's *Daremo shiranai chiisana kuni* (My secret world), and Tomoko Inui's *Kokage no ie no kobitotachi* (Yuri and the Little Folk), a new literary genre was born: the Japanese fantasy novel for children. Of course we must not forget that an important forerunner of modern fantasy had already appeared in 1947: Momoko Ishii's *Nonchan kumo ni noru* (Nonchan rides the clouds). In 1955 Riron-sha launched their Creative Literature for Children series. In the period since then, we can count many distinguished authors for children's books, such as Miyoko Matsutani, Yoshitomo Imae, Haruo Yama-shita, and others, too numerous to mention.

Also in 1955, the Japan School Association (SCLA), which was established in 1950, started an annual essay contest for school children, aimed at promoting the reading of newly published books. This contest is still being held. Ever since 1962, just before the summer vacation, an official list of fourteen books selected by SCLA for all levels from primary school to high school is announced. This automatically guarantees sales of from 50,000 to 350,000 copies per title and provides publishers with a splendid opportunity for promoting their new titles. At the same time, this competition has caused unending debates between those for and those against it. Those who favor it say that it can play an important role in encouraging children to read and enjoy the contents of new books. On the other hand, those opposed say the set selection may restrict children's taste and freedom of choice. Forcing children to read and write essays as homework could also cause

children to reject reading altogether.

In the fifties Fukuinkan Shoten gradually achieved a new importance as a discoverer and mentor of many types of new talent in the form of picture book authors and illustrators. Among them were: Chiyoko Nakatani, Yasuo Segawa, Suekichi Akaba, and Sei-ichi Horiuchi, to name only a few of those whose titles were later introduced abroad. In 1961, Fukuinkan Shoten began a series introducing world-famous picture books, including Dick Bruna's books, Beatrix Potter's Peter Rabbit books, and others of equal renown. These examples in turn stimulated many Japanese picture book authors and editors.

In 1962 Yasoo Takeichi, the founder of Shikosha, began issuing single-title picture books in addition to a monthly magazine, *Kodomo no Sekai* (Children's world), for distribution to Catholic kindergartens. His emphasis was on the pictures rather than the story, and on letting the artists think freely and express their ideas and imagination through pictures. He was most impressed with the idea behind Leo Lionni's *Little Blue and Little Yellow.* Shigeru Hatsuyama, Chihiro Iwasaki, Yutaka Sugita, Kota Taniuchi, and other artists were encouraged to draw imaginative books, and Kota Taniuchi was especially successful at expressing his own unique poetic world. These works expanded the readership of Shikosha books from children to adults. From the first stage, Takeichi showed a positive interest in international co-production of picture books. Each spring, he held an exhibition of original illustrations by internationally known picture book artists with the cooperation of Maruzen, a book importer, and a chain of bookstores.

Other children's book publishers such as Kaiseisha, Iwasaki Shoten, and Akane Shobo became active and followed in the footsteps of Fukuinkan Shoten and Shikosha. Reasons behind their success were, of course, the economic growth of Japan at the time and "the second baby boom," following World War II, in addition to the energetic activities of the publishers themselves. These phenomena combined to present artists, graphic designers, illustrators, and cartoonists with manifold opportunities and places to express their imagination.

One of the most distinguished of the author-illustrators to emerge was Mitsumasa Anno, who made his debut with his first book of Escher-like pictures, *Fushigina E,* in 1968. His way of thinking was influenced by geometry, mathematics, and the other sciences. These interests combined with his artistic ability to create a remarkable world of illusion. He always hides something in his pictures to give the pleasure of discovery and stimulate the imagination, as in the series of his Journey books (published by Fukuinkan Shoten), and his more recent *Flea Market* (Dowaya).

Another important factor in the growth of children's books in the late sixties and in the seventies has been the diversification of markets, which were extended to include door-to-door sales, specialized children's bookstore activities, and sales to the home library movement.

Momoko Ishii is an author, editor, and translator of books for young readers who might be called the Anne Carroll Moore of Japan, though she is not a librarian. Since she wished for greater contact with the actual children who were her readers, she established a library at her home in 1958. The idea caught on, and similar home libraries gradually spread throughout Japan, reaching a peak in about 1979. Today, these private libraries number close to five thousand.

In a way, the flourishing home library movement is rather embarrassing, for it points up the inadequacies of library services for children. As of 1985 there were 1,633 public libraries in Japan; of these, 1,127 had children's sections. Even so, the figures represent a heartening improvement over those of fifteen years previously: in 1970, among 881 public libraries, only 358 had children's sections. Paradoxically, the inadequacy of library service may also have encouraged the flourishing of the retail book trade. There are nearly 13,000 bookshops today in Japan, which range from large outlets in cities to small family-run neighborhood shops. The specialist children's bookshops now total 73.

Another new sales development was the door-to-door sales campaign, conducted by Holp Books in Tokyo, Japan Book Loan in Kobe, and other similar companies in 1975 and for several years after. Holp Books aimed to distribute sets of translated picture books published by Holp Shuppan, as well as original Japanese works, as a set of twenty-four to thirty volumes targeting three age groups, from preschool through primary school. Imported picture books in original languages were well accepted by mothers or teachers whose higher education equipped them to read English or other languages. This marked the beginning of an amazingly successful program which naturally tended to cause overseas publishers to regard Japan as a superlative market for original language edition picture books and translated picture books.

These successes encouraged other children's book publishers who had previously concentrated only on works by Japanese authors and artists, and they began to show interest in publishing translations of overseas picture books. Publishers without children's divisions took a second look at the possibilities of children's book publishing and in some cases expanded their firms so as to enter the juvenile market. Large corporations outside the publishing field also started publishing translated editions of picture books; some firms, like CBS-Sony, aimed at an audience of young adults.

This boom, however, did not last for more than six years, and many translated children's books have since disappeared through a process of natural selection, as some publishers who entered this field have, too.

In recent years, door-to-door sales operations have become notorious and increasingly regarded with suspicion after certain large-scale door-to-door enterprises were found to have been swindling people. By this time, too, most families already have enough

encyclopedias or book sets.

In the 1980s there has been a growing interest in comics for children, resulting in a combined circulation of more than 7.5 million copies for the top five magazines. Picture books based on television's animated cartoons or on biographical TV programs have been quite popular since 1979. Some mass-market publishers issued "secret" series, with answers to questions given by popular TV and comics characters. These have been accepted quite well by younger children. The combination of the comics and education in Gakushu Manga, or "educational comics," was an innovation from Shueisha, soon to be followed by other publishers both mass-market and serious. These comics presented, for instance, Japanese history in cartoons or world history in cartoons. The phrase "Kei Haku Tan Sho," which means "light, thin, short, and small" — lightweight and lacking in substance, we might say — has become fashionable as a key-word expressing the nature of present social phenomena and the temper of the times. This penchant for the lightweight is not limited to children's book publishing but is also found in the adult world at large in today's Japan.

In the storybook field, easy-to-read (light) or nonsense books have sold increasingly well. Most publishers attempt to balance such titles with more serious ones, also making efforts to attract good readers. Some publishers and distributors set up book fairs for works by certain authors, such as Kenjiro Haitani, whose *Usagi no me* (Rabbit's eyes) and *Taiyo no Ko* (The child of the sun) were best-sellers. Very serious fiction or nonfiction on themes such as the atomic bomb, World War II, or problems of handicapped children have also sold well, owing to vigorous promotion by the publishers and distributors.

One noteworthy event was the establishment of a paperback series known as Four Bunko (Quartet library). This was formed jointly by four publishers to promote and distribute their titles in a uniform-design softcover edition. Individual success might have been difficult but the joint effort has proved highly competitive. After Kaiseisha Bunko (Paperback library) appeared, similar paperback libraries were launched by other publishers.

Except for those titles with the continuous support of television promotion, the life cycle of children's books has tended to become shorter. There are too many other, more attractive things like computer games, including "Family Computer Games" (in Japanese, "Famicon," which in 1986 was called "Famicon Typhoon Shock"). To accompany these computer games, game books and adventure books have become popular with children.

Educational methods have become more diversified, including computer-assisted or computer-managed instruction. The use of audiovisual educational systems is characteristic mainly of the private, entrance-exam preparatory schools called *juku,* which most children attend after regular school hours. In consequence, a whole variety of "educational tools" are now being published, including, for example, correspondence questionnaires sent through the mail or sets of educational materials to be delivered to homes. These sets combine games and instructional material, so that children can study and at the same time amuse themselves. Some of these educational materials and certain educational comics are included in the figures given in the table.

In my opinion, publishing in Japan today has arrived at a stage which can be called a turning point for the children's book field. Those publishers who have been publishing comics and "lightweight" projects are doing well, while those whose aim is the production of good, serious books are in decline. They face a serious dilemma: although they have a strong desire to publish "good" books for children, to compete for survival they must also publish "light" books as well. The tendency of "Kei Haku Tan Sho" or "Keicho Fuhaku" (fickle and frivolous) is apparent in every field, regardless of age, which means that "serious, grand, long, thick" — solid and substantial — things are less acceptable. I do hope, however, that the trees will grow healthily. Someone once told me that the reader's taste changes in seven-year cycles.

In concluding, please let me add a few words from the standpoint of a literary agent hoping for a cultural bridge between East and West. When I started to introduce overseas children's books to Japanese publishers in 1975, there was, in the main, only one-way traffic — in the lane to Japan. At present, however, I am proud to say that we have traffic moving both ways. One reason for this may be the influence foreign works introduced to Japan have had on Japanese picture book authors and editors. Thanks to the efforts and interest of American editors who appreciate Japanese works, there are now many picture books and photographic books from Japan on the U.S. market. Soon I hope there will be a similar upswing of overseas interest in Japanese children's novels.

Japanese Publishing, Public Libraries, and Schools, 1970–1986

Year	New Books Published	Children's Books	Publishers	Bookshops	Public Libraries	Schools
1970	18,754	1,407	2,561	8,579	881	60,782
1971	20,158	1,493	2,748	8,654	885	60,791
1972	20,670	1,647	2,883	8,886	915	60,850
1973	20,446	1,421	2,894	9,339	950	61,988
1974	20,278	1,838	2,988	9,580	989	62,548
1975	22,858	2,449	3,098	10,132	1,048	62,993
1976	24,913	2,754	3,170	10,641	1,083	63,410
1977	26,690	3,256	3,224	11,006	1,113	64,073
1978	27,150	2,700	3,704	11,427	1,199	64,631
1979	27,132	2,667	4,092	11,741	1,320	65,164
1980	27,709	2,466	4,269	12,144	1,362	65,533
1981	29,263	2,598	4,154	12,251	1,444	65,778
1982	31,523	2,713	4,327	12,507	1,487	65,883
1983	33,617	2,727	4,231	12,719	1,569	66,033
1984	35,853	3,007	4,169	12,861	1,642	66,119
1985	35,920	3,065	4,183	12,985	1,633	66,136
1986	35,752	2,688	4,258	13,024	1,694	66,057

Source: Shuppan Kagaku Kenkyujo (Institute of Publishing and Science)
Shuppan News (Publishing news)

The Japanese Children's Book Collection at the Library of Congress

by TAYO SHIMA

Japanese children's books may be found in the Japanese Section of the Library of Congress, part of the Asian Division, located in the John Adams Building. The collection of contemporary children's literature, which includes fiction, nonfiction, folk literature, drama, poetry, anthologies, collections, periodicals, and criticism, is considered the largest and best outside of Japan. Although the card catalog in the Asian Section contains about fifteen hundred juvenile fiction titles, it is difficult to figure out the true extent of the Library's holdings of children's books written in the Japanese language. This is because children's books in art, history, social and political science, law, drama, and criticism are cataloged with adult works in their respective subject fields and cards for them are filed in the general card catalog. Japanese children's books represented as such in the card catalog are a selection made from works published from 1958 to 1980.[1]

All the books in this collection were selected by a selecting committee and acquired through the Tokyo representative of the Library of Congress. The chief source for selection has been the Japanese National Library's Weekly Acquisition List. The list consists of approximately eight hundred new titles, and of these two hundred were selected each week for the Library of Congress collection. This means that of the new publications in Japan the Library of Congress has traditionally acquired one-quarter. Unfortunately, with the recent drastic budget cuts, the regular acquisitions of the Japanese Section have been significantly reduced. In 1986 Japan produced 35,752 new titles and of these 2,688 were in the category of children's literature and related subjects. This is not, however, reflected in the Library's selection policy, which resulted in the selection of a mere twenty children's titles, less than 1 percent of the publications in this, Japan's most rapidly growing genre.

When the number of books selected is so small, the criteria for selection should be quite strict. At present the selection committee gives preference to those books that have received prestigious awards. Actually, Japan has more than sixty awards for children's books yearly; with so many award-winning books, additional screening methods must be used. Selectors also refer to important mass media, to reviews in major newspapers, and to publishing industry news. Occasionally, children's literature specialists in Japan have been consulted. Since children's publications in Japan are booming in quantity, if not quality, the process of selecting the best of each year's titles becomes increasingly difficult.

Unlike current children's or young adults' books published in the United States, which receive Annotated Card (AC) Cataloging in the Children's Literature Section, Japanese children's books are handled by the staff of the Japanese Section of the Shared Cataloging Division. These catalogers, who are also responsible for all other Japanese-language materials, provide no annotations or any other special treatment appropriate to the genre; a title translation into English is not even made. Thus, it is rather difficult for researchers without Japanese-language skills to become aware of the real value of this collection.

It is important to realize that the Library's collection of Japanese children's books includes far more than the scope of contemporary literature I have mentioned thus far. The fact that the collection includes some early original printings of prewar and even pre-Meiji era works shows clearly that its chronological scope is much more than the often cited 100 years. These older resources permit scholars to trace the history of Japanese children's literature back to its earliest stages. In the important tradition of the *monogatari,* stories that have been told and retold, we can see the foundations of Japanese children's literature as it is transformed in accordance with the changes in society at large.

The Library of Congress holds pre-Meiji Japanese Juvenilia in the rare book enclosure of the Japanese Section. The illustrated version of *Taketori Monogatari* (Princess Splendor),[2] probably of the seventeenth century, must be one of the most important of these holdings, because it illustrates several fascinating aspects of early Japanese reading material for children. *Princess Splendor* is a typical Japanese fairy tale about someone descended from another world, and it contains none of the didactic elements so characteristic of contemporaneous Western children's literature. In *The Tale of Genji,* the world's first novel, written in the eleventh century, *Princess Splendor* is referred to as the very first *monogatari.*[3] The monogatari is one of Japan's oldest literary forms, and it functioned as more than just a fairy tale, including at its heart elements of fantasy and the spiritual world which have been passed down from the earliest Japanese myths.

According to *The Tale of Genji, Princess Splendor* was a favorite subject for picture scrolls drawn by such distinguished figures as Kase no Ōmi and Kino Tsurayuki[4] or more often by attending court ladies for the princes and princesses in those early days. Such picture scrolls were very elaborate affairs; often the paper used was imported from China, and precious stones were carefully chosen to decorate the scroll spindle. One of the most important skills for young princesses to learn was that of knitting the silk braids used to tie the scrolls. Clearly these scrolls represent reading material carefully prepared for aristocratic children, primarily for their genuine pleasure, without an emphasis on instruction.

Another important holding of the Library of Con-

gress is a hand-written codex, *Hōmyō Dōji,* a Buddhist moral tale. This title is in the codex format developed from the earlier picture scrolls and generally called "Nara picture books." With the growth of the reading population in the fifteenth and sixteenth centuries, this codex format was created as a substitute for the expensive picture scrolls. The creation of the long and continuous illustrations of the picture scroll required extensive artistic training and skill. Folding the scroll into pages limited the size of each picture and enabled artists of lesser talent to engage in the job of illustrating stories. Thus, the handwritten codex format became a popular vehicle for illustrated stories, and it existed side by side with the picture scroll until, and even after, the advent of printing.

Through the succeeding warrior governments in Kamakura and Muromachi (twelfth through the four-teenth centuries), tales of warrior heroes and battle stories were added to the monogatari. But it was the following turmoil of civil wars (fifteenth and sixteenth centuries), when the capital, Kyoto, was often in flames and the powerful provincial clan leaders were being supplanted by their retainers, that resulted in the most productive era for stories in the entire history of Japan. In addition to romances and battle stories, there were stories about soldiers, priests, farmers, and people of all backgrounds. There were popular animal and plant stories, ghost, revenge, and rags-to-riches stories. All these came to be embodied in a literary form called *Otogizōshi,* tale-teller's books, and became a major factor in the blooming publishing scene of the ensuing Edo period.

The three hundred years of the Shogunate, from the beginning of the seventeenth century up to the Meiji Restoration of 1868 is called the Edo period, after the capital city, Edo, now Tokyo. With increasing literacy among trades and craftsmen classes, these two lower levels in the four ranks of the Edo social system played a major role in the economy, and they eventually became the substantial middle class. This middle class gave rise to the vibrant and colorful popular culture which was expressed in *Haikai* (a form of poem), *Kabuki* (theater), *Ningyō Jōruri* (puppet theater), and *Ukiyozōshi* (the novel). But unfortunately, during these three hundred years characterized by strict class distinction under pervasive Confucian morality, opportunities for adventure and romance were sealed off. Characters in stories were subject to the same rules as their living counterparts. The laws were extremely confining and even travel was restricted by means of tightly guarded checkpoints along the roads to Edo. Thus, in a strict sense, only Otogizōshi from the previous era and educational works were accepted as safe reading materials for Edo-era children.

Among the educational books of the Edo period in the Asian Division rare book collections are *Honchō Onna Kagami,* describing exemplary behavior of famous women, and *Ehon Teikin Ōrai,* an illustrated manual and guide to correct correspondence, illustrated by Hokusai, a master Ukiyo-e artist.[5] The typical Edo story is represented in the Library's holdings by *Ishidōmaru Karukaya Monogatari.*[6] It was written by Kyokutei Bakin, a talented Edo-period writer, and is illustrated by Hokusai. The story is about the journey of a boy and his mother in search of his missing father, a popular theme of Edo-period literature. It seems that only a journey in search of family or a tale of revenge for a trespass against a family member (even if it involved breaking the law of checkpoints along the roads) could escape the moral censorship of the times.

Before I begin to discuss children's books in modern Japan, let me quickly tell you two facts that might further illuminate the Edo publishing scene in relationship to children's book publication in the Western world. Just eight years after the first publication of *Orbis sensualium pictus* by Comenius in Nuremburg,

Japan produced its first picture encyclopedia. Published in 1666, *Kinmōzui* was written and illustrated by Tekisai Nakamura, in twenty chapters, in seven volumes.[7] It is said that the book was a great success and became the forerunner of this constantly popular genre on the Japanese publishing scene.

The other fact is that in the Matsuzaka area, two hundred miles southwest of Tokyo, a bundle of books was found rather recently inside a body of Jizo, a stone Buddhist guardian, god of children. This was included as a highlight in the exhibition of "The Early History of Children's Books in Japan" mounted for the 1986 IBBY Tokyo meeting.[8] These were books of heroes and animals and picture catalogs of Tengu, a long-nosed goblin, of a jester, and of bad monks. They were Akahon (Red Books), Japan's mass-produced picture books of the seventeenth century, which are quite analogous to English chapbooks, especially in terms of their widespread popularity. The bundle of books actually belonged to the son of a rich merchant who died young, and they were probably buried to obtain consolation at the boy's death. These publications from the Kyoto area of the 1660s and 1670s show that active publishing for children before the nineteenth century in Japan was not restricted to the Edo region but had a widespread geographical range. It is doubtful, though, that these Akahon were publications intended solely for children, for they contain hidden vulgar references and metaphors sometimes printed in the gutter of the pages. But it is clear that children used the little books, just as English children did their chapbooks.

In spite of the blossoming of publishing, the essence of monogatari was gradually lost through and after the Edo moral reforms. Picture books often became simply catalogs. Certain adventures and romances had long been classics, and new ones were not being openly created. The soul-seeking artists had to disguise their works under masks. Thus, people had to wait for change, the social changes that were at last to come after three hundred years of a rigid social framework and a closed society. We should not forget, however, that in this same social framework people developed the extremely subtle ways of aesthetic sensibility in both art and daily life.

The official opening of Japan and the Meiji Restoration in 1868 changed the social climate to a denial of Edo culture and inevitably brought a strong national purpose to education and publications for children in general. Nonetheless, the chaotic state of the first decade of this period resulted in a rather unusual moment of freedom from any conforming force and there was a flood of translation, mostly from Anglo-American sources. Yukichi Fukuzawa, an influential educator, introduced Western ideas in his writings, a complete collection of which may be found in the Library's general Japanese catalog. His *Gakumon no Susume* (The encouragement of learning), published in 1873, was partly an adaptation of Francis Wayland's *The Elements of Moral Science.*[9] Fukuzawa's book was published in seventeen booklets over four years and is said to have sold four million copies. Along with his *Dōmō Oshiegusa* (Instruction for a child's enlightenment), a translation of William and Robert Chambers's *Moral-Class Book* published in 1869, Fukuzawa's work was widely used in school textbooks and was accepted enthusiastically by both adults and adolescents. Thus, the immediate post-Restoration period saw a quick but brief reaction to outside civilization and enlightenment.[10]

The first children's best-seller in the Meiji period, *Koganemaru,* was written by Sazanami Iwaya in the conventional written language. It is an old moral tale of filial piety featuring an orphan puppy who avenges his father's death by vanquishing the ferocious tiger responsible for it. The Library owns a fascimile reprint of the original 1891 printing and it is the earliest prewar title listed in the bibliography *Japanese Children's Books at the Library of Congress.*[11]

Interestingly, two introductions were written for *Koganemaru,* one by Ougai Mori, a leading literary figure of Meiji, and the other by Sazanami Iwaya himself. Both referred to children's literature in European countries using words like *juvenile literature* and *Jugendshrift* in expressing their hearty commitment to this new genre. This represents the first serious acknowledgment of books for children as a separate literature. *Koganemaru* was the first of a series of twenty-five collections of stories, and it was such a success that the publisher was encouraged to continue the venture with historical, moral, and folktale books for children. These books would soon be overshadowed, however, by the growing nationalistic climate.

In the same year as the first appearance of *Koganemaru,* a translation of Frances Hodgson Burnett's *Little Lord Fauntleroy* was published in Japan.[12] The translator, Shizuko Wakamatsu, was the Christian wife of a noted school teacher, and her use of modern language was considered one of the best examples of the then-current drive to unify the written language and the vernacular. Compared with the traditional moral purpose of *Koganemaru,* whose main characters always exhibited exemplary behavior, *Little Lord Fauntleroy* portrays a child acting as a child and an individual. The translation had an impact on many Japanese minds and created an audience that could question the forthcoming flood of increasing nationalism in major commercial publications. An early edition of this translation of *Little Lord Fauntleroy* has been acquired by the Library (but it is not within the scope of the bibliography *Japanese Children's Books at the Library of Congress* because of its English-language origin).

Although throughout the periods of the Japan-China War, the Japanese-Russian War, and World War I, increasing nationalism characterized the educational and historical reading materials of Japan, a monumental phase in children's book history arrived in the form of *Akaitori* (Red bird), a new children's periodical.[13] Founded and edited by Miekichi Suzuki, a talented student of Sōseki Natsume, *Red Bird* was launched in 1918 with articles from most of the literary figures of note of that time. It was in this periodical that important cultural movements, such as free art education, the nursery rhyme revival, and a literary movement called Dōshin-shugi were presented. *Dōshin-shugi* might be defined as the literary attitude of trying to see the world through the eyes of a child.[14]

The interesting fact about the articles in periodicals like *Red Bird* was that a great many of them were taken from foreign sources, although they were not always faithful translations. Anatole France, Alphonse Daudet, Charles Louis-Philippe, Oscar Wilde, and Mark Twain were all repeatedly adapted. In some cases sources were acknowledged, but apparently the retelling of a literary work was standard practice in Japanese children's books. In many cases, however, the true literary essence of the originals was lost and in some cases the alterations were crucial. For example, a recently published study of retelling of stories in Japanese children's periodicals discusses the case of Prosper Merimée's *Mateo Falcone.* In his retelling of this work for *Red Bird,* Miekichi Suzuki completely deleted the murder of the protagonist at the climax.[15]

The pages of *Red Bird* were largely given over to readers' contributions, just as was the case with the American *St. Nicholas* magazine. Poems, artwork, and articles written by children appeared, accompanied by the selectors' comments and guidance, which surely resulted in the birth of new writers for the next generation.

These characteristics of *Red Bird* were generally reflected in other major literary periodicals such as *Dōwa* (Fairy tale) and *Kinno Fune* (Golden ship).[16] However, *Red Bird's* Miekichi Suzuki should certainly be credited with establishing the genre of children's literature by promoting a modern Japanese style in the retelling of various literary sources. A complete collection of Miekichi Suzuki's work for children is in the Library, as is a complete file of *Dōwa* magazine in facsimile reprint, as an example of Taishō-era periodicals for children. Both are also described in my bibliography of Library of Congress holdings.

If Sazanami Iwaya and Miekichi Suzuki's achievement was the introduction of a potential world of children's literature through their influential editorship as well as their preeminent art of retelling, Mimei Ogawa was one exceptional figure who devoted himself to creating his own stories. As an anarchist, Ogawa found his basic themes in social concerns, but he put them in the most fantastic settings, in his poetical style of description. Some of the loveliest and saddest stories written by Mimei Ogawa were neglected in the postwar era, and were regarded as unsuitable for children's literature because of the author's total commitment to his emotional and naive inspiration rather than to his young readers. An advocate of the Dōshin-shugi movement, his prime reason for writing stories

for children was simply that he could indulge his artistic creativity best in this genre. A complete collection of works by Mimei Ogawa is a part of the Library's holdings, and these titles are listed in the bibliography *Japanese Children's Books.*

Soon the ephemeral proletarian children's book era arrived in conjunction with the Marxist literature movement of the late twenties and early thirties. These books of the people were banned in 1932 when Japan plunged into the rabid nationalism that led to the war. Literary magazines like *Red Bird* were taken over by commercial magazines such as *Shōnen Kurabu* (Boy's club).[17] With the growing militarism, children were to be made into "little patriots" and they were given stories told in hot imperialistic tones. Unlike *Red Bird* or *Dōwa,* which were loaded with articles by noted literary figures, *Boy's Club* had a handful of popular writers who crazed the young readers with exciting stories and adventures which took them far beyond the Japanese horizon. With the country's vision of an East Asian Coprosperity Sphere, it seems that this was the very first time that these writers could realistically dream of widening their long-confined world. Of course, it did not take long for the young readers to be intoxicated with the imperialistic dream of Japan as well. The Library of Congress holds a reproduction of *Boy's Club* in three volumes, published in 1974, as well as large numbers of uncataloged publications from the wartime and immediate postwar period, which were confiscated during the U.S. occupation of Japan.

The end of World War II brought Japan radical social change, transforming its government from imperial absolutism to a democracy. Because it represented not merely a political form but a deeply ingrained set of social values as well as religious beliefs, the fall of imperial absolutism caused the greatest dislocation of society to occur in Japan's modern history. The total confusion inevitably visited on the "little patriot" generation was crucial. The consequent vulnerability created in young minds by the experience has not yet been sufficiently examined. What we can observe is their earnest literary activity, which manifests the generation's own painstaking quest for identity.

Since the war, the mainstream of Japanese children's literature has consistently emphasized realism and thus has produced an extensive number of realistic novels. Instead of the artistic emphasis typical of the Taisho era or the nationalistic tone of the previous wartime era, the postwar writers are committed to pursuing several important goals. Writing fiction for children was the natural result of the drawn-out struggle to establish a modern Japanese style, and writing about peace and against war was an unavoidable consequence of the authors' wartime experiences and their daily exposure to the country's physical damage.

The cause of justice for children as they face their contemporary problems, such as severe competition in school, parents' divorce, and loneliness, has been quickly defended by these children's book writers and their successors. I shall leave the details to the bibliography, *Japanese Children's Books at the Library of Congress,* which covers the most important of these postwar works. Recently, however, the unrelenting emphasis on realism seems to be lifting. *Majo no Takkyubin* (Special delivery of Kiki, the witch) by Eiko Kadono, surprisingly enough a writer of the "little patriot" generation, was the winner of three major children's literature awards in 1985 and announced clearly the arrival of a new age after the postwar ordeal.[18] This little fantasy book contrasts with the realism of most "little patriot" writers.

For the first time in many ages, Japan is now enjoying freedom of expression. Japanese children's literature may be about to rediscover the long lost fantastical world of monogatari.

NOTES

1. At present, cards for titles for children published before 1958 are filed in a catalog located in the center aisle, deck 6, John Adams Building; uncataloged items published since 1980 may be traced by computer.

2. *Taketori Monogatari* (Princess Splendor) is known by several titles, the most well-known variant being "The Bamboo Cutter," the title used by Edward G. Seidensticker. See Murasaki Shikibu, *The Tale of Genji,* translated by Edward G. Seidensticker (New York: Knopf, 1976).

3. In his translation, Seidensticker refers to "Princess Splendor" as "the ancestor of all romances" (chapter 17, "A Picture Contest"), whereas the original Japanese used the term *monogatari.* Ibid., p. 311.

4. Ibid., p. 312.

5. Ryo Asai, *Honchō Onna Kagami,* is a wood-block book of twelve chapters in six volumes (Kyoto: Yoshida Shiroemon, 1661). Hokusai Katsushika, *Ehon Teikin Ōrai,* is a wood-block book in one volume; the year it dates from is unknown.

6. Bakin Kyokutei, *Ishidōmaru Karukaya Monogatari,* is a wood-block book dating from 1831, with five chapters in five volumes, illustrated by Hokusai.

7. Teiji Seta, *Ochibo Hiroi,* 2 vols. (Tokyo: Fukuinkan-shoten, 1982), vol. 1, pp. 68-69.

8. Japanese Board on Books for Young People (JBBY), Joint Program Committee for the 20th IBBY Congress, comp., *Nihon no kodomo no hon rekishi ten: Jūshichi-seiki kara jūkyū-seiki no eiribon o chushin ni* (Tokyo: JBBY/Tokyo Metropolitan Culture Foundation, 1986), pp. 23-24, 49-50.

9. Yukichi Fukuzawa, *Gakumon no Susume* (1871-75), in *Fukuzawa Yukichi Zenshu,* vol. 3 (Tokyo: Iwanami-shoten, 1969); Francis Wayland, *The Elements of Moral Science* (Boston: Gould, Kendall, and Lincoln, 1845).

10. Yukichi Fukuzawa, *Dōmō Oshiegusa* (1870), in *Fukuzawa Yukichi Zenshu,* vol. 3; William Chambers and Robert Chambers, *The Moral-Class Book* (Edinburgh: William and Robert Chambers, 1839).

11. Sazanami Iwaya, *Koganemaru,* illustrated by Keishū Takeuchi (Tokyo: Hakubundan, 1891).

12. Frances Hodgson Burnett, *Little Lord Fauntleroy,* translated by Shizuko Wakamatsu (Tokyo: Jogaku-zasshi-sha, 1889).

13. *Akaitori,* a monthly edited by Miekichi Suzuki, was published in Tokyo by Akaitori-sha, July 1918-June 1929, January 1931-October 1936.

14. Saburo Kuwabara, *Akai Tori no Jidai: Taishō no Jidō Bungaku* (Tokyo: Keio-tsushin, 1975), p. 258.

15. Motoko Satō, *Ienakiko no Tabi* (The journey of Sans Famille) (Tokyo: Heibon-sha, 1987).

16. *Dōwa,* a monthly, edited by Shōzō Chiba (Tokyo, Kodomo-sha), April 1920-July 1926; *Kinno Fune,* a monthly edited by Sajirō Saitō (Tokyo, Kin-no-tsuno-sha), November 1919-May 1922.

17. *Shōnen Kurabu,* a monthly edited by Kenichi Katō (Tokyo, Kōdansha), 1914-46.

18. Eiko Kadono, *Majo no Takkyubin,* illustrated by Akiko Hayashi (Tokyo: Fukuinkan-shoten, 1985).

108364

LIBRARY
COLBY-SAWYER COLLEGE
NEW LONDON, NH 03257

Japan's Educational Television for Children: From "Sesame Street" to "Hirake Ponkiki"

by KŌICHIRO NODA

The topic of Japanese children and television is a broad one, to which I will here try to give you a general introduction. I hope to interest you in the subject and offer to be of further help in the future, if you wish.

The first broadcasting network in Japan, NHK or Nippon Hoso Kyokai, a government-controlled nationwide radio network, was established in 1925. It was not until after the war, in 1951, that commercial broadcasting companies appeared. Today, NHK occupies two networks, one general and one educational; Broadcasting University has one network; and Satellite television has two channels. All these are public broadcasting networks. There are also five commercial television networks broadcasting today — three major ones, one smaller, and one very small. For seventeen years I worked for one of the major commercial networks, Fuji Telecasting Company, and then, twelve years ago, I established Japan Television Workshop Company.

In Japan, the rate of television ownership is almost as high as it is in America. Yet there is a big difference. The Japanese are far poorer than Americans. Although people overseas describe Japan as a prosperous country that overcame the disaster of the war in a very short time and although statistics show that Japan's Gross National Product is second in the world, after America, these statistics do not explain our standard of living.

In such little mountainous islands, in size only one-fifteenth of the United States, there live people numbering about half of the American population. You cannot imagine until you live there. We have to work very hard to survive, no matter how bad a reputation we get. We are scarcely living, working as hard as we know how, though we are scornfully labeled workaholics.

It is true that recently we Japanese have been enjoying the biggest consumption rate in our history. But this abundance is just a facade. To buy a house is now only a dream for even a high salaried businessman in an urban area. Such a person can buy cars, household goods, electric appliances, or clothes, but not a house. He can enjoy fine food at home and in restaurants. You might say, "Then, he should save that money to buy a house." But no, houses are unbelievably expensive now. It is like a child saving five or ten cents to buy a ten-speed bicycle. So, most of us give up saving money for a house and just try to get an easy materialistic enjoyment out of life. Half of Japanese fathers spend Sunday sitting in a small dining room watching television, very tired. This is the reality of Japan.

Therefore it is no wonder that television has much more to do with our daily life than is true for Americans. And children are no exception. Today, Japanese children experience a materialistic affluence that their parents did not enjoy in their own childhoods. Japanese parents spare no expense for their children. They wish to give them the best education, toys, clothes, and food. They do not want their children to know the same poverty they experienced as children.

Thus the market for children is very big and industries carry on hot sales campaigns for children's products. Television plays a very big part in their publicity efforts, and its programs and commercial messages targeted to children are very significant to such industries.

What kind of children's programs do those sponsors buy to air their commercial messages during prime

time? Most of these TV programs were made into theatrical films, or vice versa. There is a great variety of programs. Some are educational, some are heartwarming, and some are wild and crazy. Of course, among these programs are some which were not welcomed by parents and teachers. Most sponsors simply need a high viewer rate for their sales. Bad money sometimes expels good money, as you know.

On the other hand, children aren't as simple as that. There is a popular excuse among children when they are chided for their fighting; they say, "We were just copying TV action scenes." Television is sometimes accused of provoking children's violence. But children are not that simple. Television is now a requisite for their life but they are not as naive as to be dominated by it. They are intelligent enough to control themselves. This is my observation.

Then, how are they controlling themselves? Let me go on to describe the situation of Japanese children and television based on the latest research. In April 1987 an organization called the Institute of Child Research sent out questionnaires on children eight to nine years old, in an urban area.

To the question, "How often do you watch your favorite program?" 17 percent answered, "Never miss," and 26 percent indicated, "Never miss, except in some special cases." Which means that those who are enslaved are only 43 percent of the total child population.

Mr. Takayama, manager of the research center, finds this number to be an indication of children's calmness toward television. Children are much more in control than is supposed.

The next three questions were about the child's manner of watching TV. The results were quite different from what our generation expected.

To the question, "Do you switch on the television even when you don't have any specific program you want to watch?" the answer was:

Yes	.	.	.	. 31%
Sometimes	.	.	. 40%
No	.	.	.	. 29%

The positive group total is 71 percent.

When asked, "Do you watch several programs at the same time, changing the station?" the reply was:

Yes	.	.	.	. 15%
Sometimes	.	.	. 40%
No	.	.	.	. 52%

The positive group total is 55 percent.

When asked "Do you watch TV while reading books or playing with others?" children responded:

Yes	.	.	.	. 15%
Sometimes	.	.	. 42%
No	.	.	.	. 37%

The positive group total is 57 percent.

These high rates of positive response to the last three questions were a surprise to the people of our generation. For children, television must be a kind of roommate. This tendency shows a big gap between our generation and theirs. We find our information sources mainly in printed media, while children find theirs in a visual medium.

I am not saying that they have lost their habit of reading books. When I say books I do not include comic books. Today's children are reading books much more than we did.

Besides producing television programs, I have written and translated hundreds of books, including the Star Wars series and the Conan series. And my observation is that children are reading much more today than they did twenty years ago, despite the widespread watching of television programs.

How do you find all these research results?

Are Japanese children quite different from American children, or about the same? The relation between children and television must be fundamentally the same in both countries, but in Japan everything is on a smaller scale and changes occur at a quicker pace. Fashion quickly spreads throughout the small country but is also soon forgotten. The fanatical influence is stronger in Japan, I believe.

To turn to Japanese children's educational programs, I will describe Nippon Hoso Kyokai. NHK devotes one channel exclusively to educational programs for school students to watch in class during the school day and later at home. During the evening, they broadcast educational programs for adults.

Commercial broadcasters have always targeted preschoolers in their morning programming, the type of educational program that I produce. The hours from nine to eleven in the morning are one of the least expensive time periods for airing programs, and so all the children's educational programs were scheduled for those hours, and all these programs were alike. A young lady led dances, sang, or did handicrafts with children. Similar to "Captain Kangaroo" or "Romper Room," these programs did not arouse even the enthusiasm of their own producers and directors in Japan.

Then, in the early 1970s this started to change. Fuji Telecasting Company, where I worked, had been airing a children's program called "Pin Pon Pan." Since children's programs were not a big concern for the company, the director was either young and inexperienced or old and expected to retire soon. But one day a young but able director with experience with musical shows for prime time was hired. He adopted for the program a children's song written and composed by a composer who was not a specialist in children's songs. This was the "Pin Pon Pan Dance," or "Pin Pon Pan Exercise," an epoch-making song. Why? Because it became a million seller. No one expected this, since the sales of these kind of songs had normally been very low. The record company within the Fuji Television group never thought of keeping its copyright and so had canceled it. One of our rival companies made a big profit.

But this big success brought children's programs a citizenship of their own. We recognized that children's programs could be a business, and this is very Japanese. Business possibility is the biggest concern of Japanese commercial broadcasters.

Then, a new type of children's program came from America. Yes, that was "Sesame Street." We received a big shock. Everything was so fresh. It was amazing that education by visual images could be so much fun.

At the time, I was producing a children's singing contest. I made one of the biggest hits in the history of television. Since the children's songs were mostly imitations of adult songs, the PTA protested and a big controversy arose. My nephew, then a kindergarten

child, asked me, "Why can't you make an interesting program like 'Sesame Street'?" I could not say a word.

I will not go into the details that followed, but in 1973, I finally planned, produced, and directed a new children's educational program, "Hirake Ponkiki," to be telecast thirty minutes each morning from Monday to Friday. Today, it is still running on nationwide TV.

As you know, earlier children's programs were focused more toward emotional aspects of learning, whereas "Sesame Street" stressed learning through recognition. The Fuji Telecasting Company succeeded in their campaign to provide both emotional and intellectual content for children through a series of programs, "Pin Pon Pan" and "Hirake Ponkiki." Because of these shows, we enjoyed a very good reputation.

The daily program includes eight categories: Nature and People, Language, Social Life, Understanding Signs, Number and Quantity, Grouping and Distinction, Discipline, and Sense and Rhythm. These categories were created by a group headed by Dr. Azuma and his colleagues from Tokyo University. The program was highly regarded and received most of the prizes related to TV programs in Japan and also received a Silver Prize in the New York Television and Film Festival in 1983 and the prize for TV programs for children from the Asia Pacific Broadcasting Union in 1984.

In 1975 one incident that took place concerning "Hirake Ponkiki" left a monument not only in Japanese broadcasting history but also in the history of Japanese culture.

One song in the program made an unprecedented hit with more than five million record sales. Of course, its sales could not rival Bing Crosby's "White Christmas," but it is still one of the biggest hits in the world's record sales. Even now, the biggest sales figure for adult songs in Japan is only two million. You can imagine, then, what a big hit it was.

The song was "Oyoge Taiyakikun" or in English, "Swim! Master Taiyaki." *Taiyaki* is a traditional Japanese sweet, which is a kind of waffle shaped like a fish and stuffed with sweet mashed beans.

Master Taiyaki was not happy to think about his short life. These sweets are doomed to be eaten very soon: no fun, no liberty, no life. Master Taiyaki ventures to flee away to the sea, where he finds how wonderful life is. Soon, however, he is caught by a man and quickly eaten. The song became very popular not only with children but also with many adults and businessmen, who just work and work, and have no fun, no liberty. At the 1975 year-end parties, people sang this song together all over the country.

This hit brought a new ten-story building to the record company but not to the television network. We were very satisfied, however, that we had created a turmoil in the history of television and once again had encouraged broadcasters to make children's programs better.

The song triggered an avalanche of imitations of "Ponkiki" by other TV companies, including NHK. But all the imitations disappeared within three years. Today there are only two children's educational programs left: our "Hirake Ponkiki" and NHK's old-fashioned program.

Now perhaps you can understand how difficult it is for commercial broadcasters in Japan to make children's educational programs. They cannot exist without being profitable, though this word may offend some of you. At the same time, children are not as naive as to be controlled by adults' intentions when the program is not built on a valid concept or a curriculum based on a full study and observation of the responses of children.

In conclusion, I would like to say that Japanese children—though they live in such a densely populated environment and face such a concentration of information and study — have enough adaptability to live a better life. Nature gives children the wisdom to adapt. I would be very happy if my words could be an incentive for you to become interested in Japanese children and in Japan itself.

Note: Tapes of "Hirake Ponkiki" shown by Kōichiro Noda at the time he gave this talk are available through the Children's Literature Center.

An Imagination-Stretching Adventure: Editing the Works of Mitsumasa Anno in the U.S.A.

by ANN BENEDUCE

Mitsumasa Anno, winner of the 1984 Hans Christian Andersen Medal and many other national and international awards, began his professional life as a teacher in a private school. A man of many talents and interests, Mr. Anno shared his enthusiasm for art, nature, history, literature, mathematics, and travel with his students. Among them were the children of Tadeshi Matsui, director of Fukuinkan Shoten, one of the largest and most distinguished publishers of children's books in Japan. His children were so excited by their wonderful teacher that Mr. Matsui felt he had to meet him, and from this meeting came both friendship and a career of creating beautiful, imaginative books. In 1968 Mitsumasa Anno's first book, *Fushigina E,* was published in Japan. In 1970 it was brought out in the United States by Weatherhill publishers under the title *Topsy-Turvies.*

International acclaim came to Anno only a few years later, with the appearance of *Anno's Alphabet,* published in the United States in 1974 by the T. Y. Crowell Company, where I was the head of the children's book department. This stunningly original book was the first one of Mitsumasa Anno's that I was privileged to edit and publish. I well remember the events that led up to my introduction to the work of this distinguished and fascinating author and artist.

It was in March of 1973, and I was attending the International Children's Book Fair in Bologna, Italy. Tadeshi Matsui had asked both Judy Taylor (children's book editor of The Bodley Head, a British publishing house) and me to meet him at the Fukuinkan Shoten stand early on the opening day. Something special was in the air. We three had copublished several books already, with mutual pleasure and success — including the delightful *The Animals' Lullaby* by Trude Alberti, illustrated by Chiyoko Nakatani. Now Mr. Matsui could hardly conceal his elation as he produced the artwork for what was to become *Anno's Alphabet: An Adventure in Imagination.* There it was — the handsome page layouts with the block letters seemingly crafted of solid oak, but each with its intriguing trompe l'oeil effect; the delicate borders; the full-color illustrations of words beginning with the various letters. It was not yet complete, but it was clear to both Judy and me from what we saw that this was the work of a subtle and imaginative thinker as well as a masterful illustrator and designer. *Anno's Alphabet* was published with great success the following year.

At first our working relationship was necessarily filtered through his Japanese editors, since Anno's English was limited and neither Judy nor I spoke Japanese. Usually, with each new project, Judy and I would consult and agree on whatever changes might be needed for the English and American markets — then, one of us would communicate our joint suggestions or comments to the editors at Fukuinkan. There the editors would discuss our comments with Mr. Anno, and write us his responses. All this went astonishingly smoothly, considering the complexity of some of the books. Soon we all felt we were warm friends, despite the distances between us.

Then, in 1977 came the exciting news that Mitsumasa Anno would be coming through New York for a few days, en route to Europe. By this time he had a number of avid fans in the bookstores as well as the library community, so plans were made for introducing him to some of them at lunches and dinners. I volunteered to meet him at the airport and bring him to his hotel. I arrived at the airport with a copy of *Anno's Counting Book* in hand, as identification, since neither of us had seen the other before. His plane landed, and after a little time, scores of people began coming out of the exit, including a number of Japanese men. None, however, responded to my waving the book in their direction. Time passed, the crowd thinned. What had happened? Had I made a mistake in the time? Just as I was becoming completely discouraged, the door opened again and through it came Anno, whom I now recognized from his photographs. But he was flustered and upset.

He had had a problem with customs that seemed inexplicable to him. Opening his suitcase, the customs official had found in it many little cellophane packages containing a snowy, white powder. Immediately Anno, totally mystified, had been rushed off into a small room where several narcotics detectives tried to interrogate him — naturally without success! Experts opened the packets, examined the contents with suspicion and then disbelief — for they contained nothing more dangerous than soap powder! Traveling light, Anno had made neat little packages of soap so he could do his own laundry — each envelope contained just enough for one day's needs! I'm not sure he ever did understand what the problem was!

The rest of his visit went smoothly, with the help of some Japanese-American friends. Everything interested him, and his warmth, humor, and intelligence charmed all who met him. By now he was working on his delightful "journey books." *Anno's Journey* was published in 1978 — another ground-breaking book. Because it was wordless, there was a strong possibility that it might be negatively reviewed, dismissed as a "non-book." Yet it was so rich in literary reference, so

innovative in concept, and visually so appealing that I was determined to make this book available to young American readers and viewers. I need not have worried, for the book was instantly appreciated and loved by critics and public alike. It has become a modern classic. Of his travels, Anno told me: "I wandered from town to town, from country to country, and sometimes my journey was hard. . . . By the end . . . I realized that I had set out not to collect information but . . . to discover the world . . . a world filled with variety."

A deep appreciation of the world and its peoples has permeated Anno's books for children and adults. He is a master of many artistic styles and techniques, creating books that bridge the gap between East and West.

Anno's Journey was followed by other journey books — *Anno's Italy, Anno's Britain* — as well as by books of other kinds: *The King's Flower,* a fable; *Anno's Animals,* a picture-puzzle book of hidden animals; *Anno's Medieval World,* an innovative view of history; and *Anno's Magical ABC,* a book using the visual device of anamorphosis; *Anno's Counting House,* a game-like introduction to counting, using die-cut pictures; as well as a book of his adult artwork: *The Unique World of Mitsumasa Anno.* Finally, in response to much urging on my part, he agreed to do *Anno's U.S.A.*

By this time we had become firm friends. We had met several more times in Bologna and in England and had, of course, corresponded frequently over the years. So it was natural for this particular book to be a collaboration. Letters and plans flew back and forth. His view of our history was characteristically unconventional — he proposed to tell our country's story in reverse. The central character, a man on horseback, would explore the country west-to-east, reversing the actual sequence of its development, and would move somewhat backward in time also, finally departing at the end from Plimoth Plantation just as Columbus's flagship appeared over the horizon! I loved this idea — it gave a fresh perspective to a rather familiar subject. His knowledge of our culture was incredibly deep, particularly of our popular culture — folklore, and films, but also our literature and history.

Certain parts of the country he considered "musts": California, Texas, New Mexico, New Orleans, Washington, New York, Philadelphia, Boston. He wanted to visit Mark Twain's birthplace, and Walt Whitman's and Thomas Edison's. I happily volunteered to show him around the eastern part of the country, and in the fall of 1983 he arrived. We viewed New York through his fresh eyes, from Trinity Churchyard to the top of the World Trade Center, from the New York Public Library at 42d Street to the Bronx Zoo. From my house in Princeton we drove to Edison's home and laboratory and then spent an afternoon at a harvest festival at a local apple orchard, complete with hayrides and country fiddlers. The next day we drove to Philadelphia, where we inspected the Liberty Bell and Independence Hall and other picturesque spots, even taking a ride in a horse-drawn buggy. "Nice day. Happy day," he commented.

But when we got back to my car, we discovered a thief had broken into the trunk and stolen both our cameras! Worse, Anno's passport had been in his camera case, and so it had been stolen, too! Not to mention all the photographs he had taken over the past few days! Panic! His camera was insured (mine also), and he had brought a back-up camera with him, but the passport had to be replaced. There was nothing to do but drive to New York and persuade the Japanese consulate to issue him a new one. This accomplished, however, he was in a celebratory mood. "New passport, new person!" he said, and took me out to a wonderful Japanese dinner to mark the event. As for the lost films, he assured me the pictures were all in his head — and so they were.

We then drove to Boston, where Paul and Ethel Heins made sure he saw all the important historical sites and monuments and also made him welcome at dinner. Their home appears in the book, as does mine, along with Tasha Tudor's lovely "Corgi Cottage," where we went next. These two artists became dear friends at first sight. As we drove up to the house, Tasha had just finished milking her goats and greeted us in a long, homespun dress, her feet bare, with a pail of milk in each hand. Even barefoot, she looked enchanting. Anno had never seen anything like her house, filled with authentic early American furniture, and he was ecstatic. After some particularly delicious New England home cooking, Anno spent the evening showing her how to do complex origami and singing songs from his childhood.

I could not accompany Anno on the rest of his trip — to the south and west. His plan was to rent a car and simply drive around the country with his sketchbook and camera. He was stunned to discover how vast the distances were. I was able to persuade him to fly across the longer stretches at least, but he still persisted in doing a lot of driving, telephoning frequently, and sending postcards and sketches as he traveled. I smile as I turn the pages of *Anno's U.S.A.*, remembering humorous anecdotes he told about nearly every place it portrays.

It is hard to write briefly about Mitsumasa Anno, as his interests are so remarkably diverse. Nature, art, history, antiques, travel, literature — all on a worldwide scale — are some of the subjects of his fascinated study. In addition to these, he is intensely interested in science,

particularly in mathematics. These are all interests I share, which has made our years of working together exceptionally congenial. He believes that children are natural mathematicians, and that they enjoy thinking mathematically until adults somehow frighten them by making the simple seem complex. Starting with *Anno's Counting Book,* surely a masterpiece of the genre, he has produced a remarkable group of books designed to correct this situation and to return the fun to the subject. Some are simple, meant for very young children, and some are more advanced, dealing with such concepts as factorials, combinatorial analysis, and computer logic. All are brilliantly clear as well as entertaining. These mathematical books require the most careful attention in translating from Japanese to English, and I find this a fascinating intellectual challenge.

Now this many-sided genius is moving into new areas of communication. The accidental discovery at a flea market in France of a set of books by the naturalist Jean H. Fabre, with the original illustrations, sent Anno on a new journey to uncover the facts of Fabre's life and work. This has become a television film, developed by Anno. But books for children will not be forgotten. In fact, new inspiration has been provided by his grandson and granddaughter, both born within the last few years. They are much beloved by their famous grandfather Mitsumasa Anno, who, despite the demands made on him by his worldwide success, remains very much a warm and accessible human being.

Working with this remarkable and multitalented man has certainly been one of the highlights of my career as an editor and a continuing "imagination-stretching adventure," as his books have often been for his many readers.

Contributors

Ann Beneduce has been an editor in the field of children's books for more than twenty-five years, working as editor-in-chief of several large publishing houses. Since 1973, she has been Mitsumasa Anno's American editor. At present, she is a consulting editor working with Orchard Books (a division of Franklin Watts, Inc.) and also with Picture Book Studio.

Sybille A. Jagusch, chief of the Children's Literature Center at the Library of Congress and organizer of the symposium, is the editor of *Stepping Away from Tradition: Children's Books of the Twenties and Thirties* (Library of Congress, 1988) and *Japanese Children's Books at the Library of Congress,* the companion bibliography to this collection of essays.

Akiko Kurita is a literary agent, translator, and director of the Japan Foreign-Rights Centre. She has translated a number of English-language picture books into Japanese. Her autobiography, *A Treasure Box with Dreams,* was published in 1986 by Kokudosha.

Kyōko Matsuoka is known the world over as the director of the Tokyo Children's Library. She is also a storyteller, translator, and author of several children's books, including *Kushami, kushami, ten no megumi* (Sneezes, sneezes, heavenly blessings), a collection of short tall tales published by Fukuinkan Shoten in 1967.

Kōichiro Noda, writer, translator, collector of science fiction, and expert on space exploration, is the founder and president of Japan Television Workshop Company, Ltd. As a director of Fuji TV Network, he produced "Hirake Ponkiki," one of the most successful educational television programs for children in Japan today.

J. Thomas Rimer is currently chairman of the department of Hebrew and East Asian languages at the University of Maryland, College Park. He writes on a variety of subjects concerning Japan, including modern literature and the theater of all periods. His books include *Modern Japanese Fiction and Its Traditions* (Princeton University Press, 1978) and *From the Country of Eight Islands* (Anchor Books, 1981). From 1983 to 1986, Dr. Rimer was chief of the Asian Division of the Library of Congress.

Tayo Shima is the compiler of *Japanese Children's Books at the Library of Congress: A Bibliography of Books from the Postwar Years, 1946-1985* (Library of Congress, 1988). She directs an art gallery called Galérie Musée Imaginaire in Tokyo.

The script type used in this booklet is Legend, designed in Germany by F. H. E. Schneidler, and was cast by the Bauer Foundry in 1937. The body type was designed in Italy, 1495, by Francesco Griffo for the great editor and printer, Aldus Manutius. This version of that type is called Bembo and was cut in England by Monotype, 1929. Another display type used here is Lutetia, designed by Jan VanKrimpen of the Netherlands. Composition is by Acorn Press, Rockville, Maryland, and General Typographers, Washington, D.C. The booklet was designed by John Michael, Rockville, Maryland.